A Note to Pa[rents]

DK READERS is a compelling program for beginning readers, designed in conjunction with leading literacy experts, including Dr. Linda Gambrell, Director of the School of Education at Clemson University. Dr. Gambrell has served on the Board of Directors of the International Reading Association and as President of the National Reading Conference.

Beautiful illustrations and superb full-color photographs combine with engaging, easy-to-read stories to offer a fresh approach to each subject in the series. Each DK READER is guaranteed to capture a child's interest while developing his or her reading skills, general knowledge, and love of reading.

The five levels of DK READERS are aimed at different reading abilities, enabling you to choose the books that are exactly right for your child:

Pre-level 1: Learning to read
Level 1: Beginning to read
Level 2: Beginning to read alone
Level 3: Reading alone
Level 4: Proficient readers

The "normal" age at which a child begins to read can be anywhere from three to eight years old, so these levels are only a general guideline.

No matter which level you select, you can be sure that you are helping your child learn to read, then read to learn!

LONDON, NEW YORK, MUNICH,
MELBOURNE, AND DELHI

Produced by Southern Lights
Custom Publishing

For Dorling Kindersley
Publisher Andrew Berkhut
Executive Editor Andrea Curley
Art Director Tina Vaughan
Photographer Howard L. Puckett

Reading Consultant
Linda Gambrell, Ph.D.

First American Edition, 2001
05 10 9 8 7 6 5 4
Published in the United States by DK Publishing, Inc.
375 Hudson Street, New York, New York 10014

Published in Great Britain by Dorling Kindersley Limited

Library of Congress Cataloging-in-Publication Data

Hayward, Linda
  A day in the life of a dancer / by Linda Hayward. -
1st American ed.
    p. cm. -- (Dorling Kindersley readers)
  Audience:"Level 1, preschool-grade 1."
  ISBN 0-7894-7370-4—ISBN 0-7894-7369-0 (pbk.)
  1. Ballet--Juvenile literature. 2.Dance Schools-Juvenile
literature.[1. Ballet dancing.] I. Title. II. Series.

GV1787.5 .H39 2001
792.8--dc21   00-055523

Printed and bound in China by L. Rex Printing Co., Ltd.

The characters and events in this story are fictional and do not
represent real persons or events. The author would like to
thank E. J. Lopresti for her help. Special thanks to Libba Owen
and the Alabama Ballet.

All other images © Dorling Kindersley
For further imformation see: www.dkimages.com

Discover more at
www.dk.com

A Day in
the Life of
a Dancer

Written by Linda Hayward

DK Publishing, Inc.

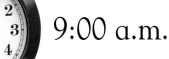

9:00 a.m.

leotard

Lisa Torres
fills her bag.

Leg warmers.
Leotard.
Tights.
Four pairs
of shoes.

4

Lisa is
a dancer.

5

Lisa walks to the ballet company.

9:30 a.m.

In the locker
room, she puts
on her toe
shoes.

toe shoes

Before class,
Lisa warms up
at the barre.

barre

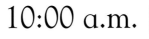 **10:00 a.m.**

The teacher comes
into the studio.
The class is practicing
ballet steps.
They practice
over and over.

The teacher watches
as the dancers move.

Every part of
the body has a
place to be!

Lisa spins on the tip of her toe. The teacher says, "Keep your shoulders low!"

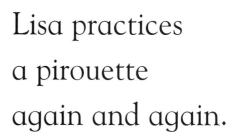

Lisa practices a pirouette again and again.

pirouette

Each step, each
movement goes
with the music.

When the class
is over, the
dancers clap.
A good teacher!

12:30 p.m.

The dancers
eat lunch and rest.
Lisa talks about her solo
in the ballet tonight.

ribbon

Lisa sees a
loose ribbon
on her shoe.
She sews it
in place.

 1:00 p.m.

Lisa puts on her tutu and goes to the studio for rehearsal.

tutu

The dance master watches as Lisa rehearses her solo. Feel the music!

Lisa has been practicing for months. She wants to do her best.

 5:00 p.m.

Lisa has a snack in the studio and thinks about being on stage. She will wear her favorite pearl earrings for good luck.

Lisa walks to the theater.
There is her roommate.
Lisa forgot her lucky pearl
earrings!

What a good friend!

STAGE

Lisa puts on her makeup and her pearl earrings.

costume

Then she puts on her costume.

8:00 p.m.

The ballet begins.
Lisa walks backstage
to wait her turn.

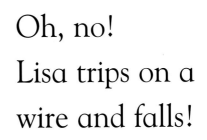

Oh, no!
Lisa trips on a
wire and falls!

Is Lisa hurt?

It is almost time
for her to dance!

Lisa stands.
She is not hurt!
She is ready
just in time.

She feels
the music
as she
walks onto
the stage.

Lisa dances
her best tonight.
She feels light
from her toes
to the tips
of her fingers!

The ballet ends.
Bravo! Bravo!
Lisa gives a
beautiful bow.

bow

10:00 p.m.

Backstage, the dance
master gives Lisa a rose.
A great performance!

Lisa and her roommate walk home together.

11:00 p.m.

It's bedtime but they can't stop talking. Lisa was so brave! The ballet was so beautiful!

Lisa thinks about her moment on stage. She smiles. She has the best job in the world!

Picture Word List

leotard
page 4

ribbon
page 15

toe shoes
page 7

tutu
page 16

barre
page 8

costume
page 20

pirouette
page 11

bow
page 28